Contents

Could you be a DJ?

To be a great DJ, you need to love music with a passion. To DJs, music is not just something to listen to – it is their life. If you love music so much that you want to share it with people, you have what it takes to be a DJ.

*Reading and understanding a crowded dancefloor from high up in a **booth** is a vital part of being a successful DJ.*

Getting it right

There are several skills you need to learn to become a DJ and play, or **mix**, tunes together. However, the first thing you need to know is that mixing is not that important. The key to being a great DJ is playing the right records at the right time. Some of the greatest DJs of all time cannot mix two records together – what set them apart were their tune, or **track**, selection and their ability to 'read a crowd'. This means knowing how to make a room full of people dance.

What format?

The three main formats used by DJs are **vinyl records**, CDs and **MP3s**. Records come in three sizes – 12-inch, 10-inch and 7-inch – and are played on a **turntable**. A lot of DJs use CDs because they are cheap and you can create your own with a home computer. An MP3 is a file format for playing music on computers and digital music players.

Master This!

DJing

Matt Anniss

WAYLAND

Published in 2012 by Wayland

Hachette Children's Books
338 Euston Road
London NW1 3BH

Wayland Australia
Level 17/207 Kent Street
Sydney NSW 2000

Commissioning editor: Jennifer Sanderson
Senior editor: Claire Shanahan
Produced by Tall Tree Ltd
Editor, Tall Tree: Jon Richards
Designer: Ed Simkins

British Library Cataloguing in Publication Data
 Anniss, Matt.
   DJ-ing. -- (Master this)
   1. Disc jockeys--Juvenile literature.
   I. Title II. Series
   780.2'3-dc22

ISBN: 9780750268196

First published in 2009 by Wayland

Printed in China

Wayland is a division of Hachette Children's Books,
an Hachette UK company.

www.hachette.co.uk

Picture credits
All photographs taken by Michael Wicks, except:
t-top, b-bottom, l-left, r-right, c-centre
cover istockphoto.com/Alex Brosa, 4 Dreamstime.com/
Aleksandr Kiriak, 6 Creasource/Corbis, 7tr Matt Anniss,
7bl Steven Henry/Corbis, 14 Matt Anniss, 18tl Johnny
Nunez/WireImage, 20bl Dreamstime.com/Kutt Niinepuu,
22bl Dreamstime.com/Adam Radosavljevic, 23t Gareth
Davies/Getty Images, 24bl Nabil Elderkin/Getty Images,
25tr istockphoto.com/Martin Hendriks, 26cl Colin
McPherson/Corbis, 26br Thuresson

The website addresses (URLs) included in this book were
valid at the time of going to press. However, because of
the nature of the Internet, it is possible that some
addresses may have changed, or sites may have changed
or closed down, since publication. While the author and
publisher regret any inconvenience this may cause the
readers, no responsibility for any such changes can be
accepted by either the author or the publisher.

Disclaimer
In preparation of this book, all due care has been
exercised with regard to the advice, activities and
techniques depicted. The publishers regret that they can
accept no liability for any loss or injury sustained. When
learning a new hobby it is important to get expert tuition
and to follow a manufacturer's instructions.

Acknowledgements
The author and publisher would like to thank Helen
and Paul Scholey, Thomas Cresswell, Tom Jones and
Keira Wilkinson

Musical styles

What type, or **genre**, of music you play should be dictated by what you love. Most modern dance music has developed from five distinct musical styles – reggae, funk/disco, drum and bass, hip-hop and house.

For example, United Kingdom (UK) garage was born when DJs started combining the speeded-up beats of house records with big basslines from drum and bass. House music itself developed as a futuristic electronic version of disco, while early hip-hop was based on **looped-up** sections of funk and disco records. When starting out, it sometimes helps to stick to one style of music, but you should never be afraid to mix it up by playing tunes from other genres. Play what you like – there are no rules!

To become a great DJ, there are a few skills you need: a good ear, a sense of rhythm, a love of music and an ability to understand what people want at a party.

Finding great music

If you are going to take DJing seriously, then you are going to have to spend a lot of time hunting for the best music. If you truly love music, this is one of the most enjoyable parts of being a DJ.

Try before you buy

Before you buy anything, make sure you listen to it first. This is the most important rule when buying music. Luckily, there are loads of places you can hear new dance music – especially on the radio and the Internet. Check out dance music websites, message boards, blogs and online stores as often as you can. This will help you keep up to date with trends, as well as giving you ideas for tunes you would like to pick up.

You should go to your local music shop and talk to the people who work there. If you give them an idea of what sort of music you like, they will be able to point you in the direction of the best tracks.

Top tip

It is best to buy little and often. Dance music changes almost daily, and the best records are often made in limited quantities. So you have to act fast if you want to pick up the best tunes!

As you build up your music collection, keep it organised. It is no use having hundreds of tunes if you do not know where any of them are.

Star file

GRANDMASTER FLASH
DJ pioneer

While living in New York in the 1970s, American DJ and musician Grandmaster Flash was one of the driving forces behind the development of hip-hop. While playing at open-air parties, Flash invented a new way of mixing records, which he called his 'quick mix theory'. This meant using two copies of the same record to extend the dancefloor-friendly parts of songs with fast cuts and mixes.

Building a collection

If you play music using MP3s or CDs, then the best way to get hold of tunes is to download them. Although it is tempting to download things for free, this can be illegal. There are plenty of online music stores where you can buy tracks cheaply. Although it helps to have a big collection, it is much better to have 100 fantastic records than 500 mediocre ones. Try not to restrict yourself to one musical style or genre. The best DJs play the finest music, regardless of style.

Getting your equipmemt

The biggest decision for any DJ is what equipment to use – turntables, **CD decks** or a computer. The basics of mixing are the same whatever you use – the only thing that changes is the controls.

Vinyl or CD?

Using vinyl is the traditional method of DJing, although more people now use CDs. When buying equipment, get the best you can afford. The cheapest DJ gear is often poorly made and may break easily. It also sounds awful! You do not have to buy the very best equipment though – these days you can get very good turntables, CD decks and mixers (see page 9) relatively cheaply.

A CD is read by a laser inside the deck. The jog wheel controls the speed of the track.

jog wheel

CD deck

A tiny needle, called the stylus, at the end of the arm reads the groove on the surface of the record, turning it into sounds.

platter

turntable arm

pitch control fader

stylus

SL-1200 Limited

turntable

Decks and mixers

When buying turntables, choose 'direct drive' ones rather than 'belt drive'. Direct drive decks have strong motors for accurate speed adjustment. This is important when trying to mix two records together (see pages 16–17). If you decide to go with CDs, get a pair of 'table top' players. Do not worry about buying an expensive **mixer** to start with: something basic will do the trick. The controls are the same whatever mixer you buy – what you pay extra for is better sound quality. Finally, you will need a good set of headphones to help with your mixing.

Mixers

The mixer is the most important tool for a DJ. It allows DJs to blend music from two or more sound sources. All conventional mixers have a row of '**upfaders**' and a horizontal **crossfader**. The upfaders are the volume controls – one for each **channel** (the mixer shown here has four upfaders for four channels). The crossfader changes the output (the music that comes out of the speakers) from one turntable to the other.

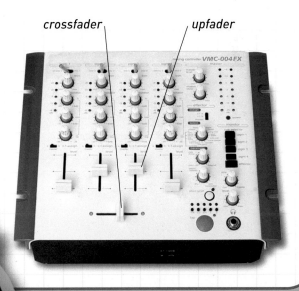

crossfader   upfader

'Close back' headphones, such as these, block out most outside noise, making mixing easier.

Top tip

Most DJ gear stockists will let you have a go on the display models, so you can get a feel for the equipment before you go ahead and buy it.

Setting up

Whether you use vinyl or CDs, the same things apply when setting up your equipment – the decks plug into the mixer, which plugs into your **amplifier**. However, you must make sure you use the correct **socket**.

Top tip

You can guard against damaging your equipment by turning everything on in the correct order. Start with the turntables or CD decks before moving onto the mixer, and finally your amplifier.

Plugging it in

Make sure all your equipment is switched off and all volume controls are set to zero. This will ensure that you do not damage your speakers. Set out your mixer between the two turntables. Each turntable needs to be connected to a separate channel on your mixer. These are represented by the upfaders, usually labelled channel 1 and channel 2, above the crossfader (see page 9).

amplifier

turntables

This is the set-up for vinyl DJing. The turntables are on either side of the mixer, which is connected to the amplifier. This is connected to the speakers.

mixer

There is a set of input sockets for each channel on the back of the mixer – usually a 'phono' input for a vinyl turntable and a 'line' input for a CD deck.

line inputs

phono inputs

output sockets

Phono or line?

You should plug your equipment into the correct input. If you connect a CD deck into a 'phono' input, the sound will distort and you may damage your equipment. Something similar will happen if you connect vinyl turntables to a 'line' input. If you are using turntables, remember to connect up the thin **ground wire** supplied with each one. This prevents static hum from ruining the music.

Once set up, the turntables need to be connected to the amplifier. This is because the sound from the mixer needs to be amplified (made louder) – you cannot plug speakers directly into your mixer.

Connecting the mixer

Plug the left-hand turntable into the channel 1 phono socket and the right-hand turntable into the channel 2 phono socket.

Connect the thin ground wire supplied with each turntable to the small screw on the back of the mixer labeled 'Ground', 'GND' or 'Earth'.

Connect one end of another phono lead to the 'Master' output sockets, and the other to the 'CD', 'Aux' or 'Tape' input on your amplifier or hi-fi.

Digital DJing

Anyone with a computer and an Internet connection can become a 'digital DJ' – all you need is a collection of tunes and some simple DJ software. If you already have a computer, getting started is easy.

Setting it up

Although you can DJ on any computer, if you plan to play at parties or in clubs, you will need a laptop that you can carry from place to place. Your laptop will also need a sound card – a device that allows you to plug your computer into a mixer. Lastly, you will need to get some DJ software.

Many computers have sound cards built into them, but you may need an external sound card, like this one.

Plugging it in

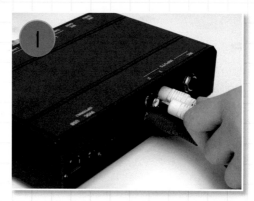

Connect the turntables to the mixer (see page 11), then connect the mixer to the sound card.

Plug one end of a **USB** cable to the output socket of the sound card.

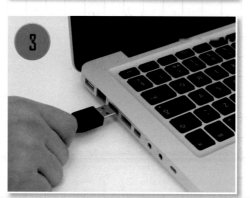

Plug the other end of the USB cable into the USB socket on your laptop.

Digital software

Perhaps the easiest place to start is with a program such as PC DJ or Virtual Turntables. These allow you to mix MP3 files on screen using your computer keyboard. You could also go for a system such as Serato Scratch or Final Scratch. These let you use a pair of vinyl turntables, two special control records and a mixer to blend music stored on your laptop. Alternatively, many DJ software packages will allow you to plug in a special digital controller – a modified mixer – to mix your music.

This set-up uses a special digital controller. It can plug directly into the computer and has its own mixing controls, so you do not need to use a mixer.

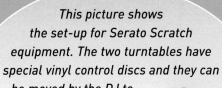

This picture shows the set-up for Serato Scratch equipment. The two turntables have special vinyl control discs and they can be moved by the DJ to control the music tracks that are stored on the laptop.

laptop

right turntable

external sound card

mixer

left turntable

Cueing

There are several techniques that you need to learn to become a great DJ. The first of these is cueing. This means listening to one track in your headphones while another is playing, to find the correct starting point.

This mixer has two upfaders, each controlling a different channel.

Mixer controls

Take a moment to familiarise yourself with the controls of your mixer. The most important controls are the channel upfaders – each with their own Cue or Pre Fade Listen (PFL) button above – and the crossfader. The two upfaders along with the crossfader allow you to mix records together. Moving the crossfader from left to right (or vice versa) while the two channel faders are pushed up, is known as cutting. This is the most basic form of mixing.

right upfader

Cue/PFL button

left upfader

crossfader

Finding the start

Before you can cut between one record and another, you need to cue up the second one and find its first beat (see below). Once you have it, keep hold of the record. When you are ready to play the track, release the record with a little push. This is known as slip-cueing and is one of the most important skills a vinyl DJ needs to learn. Slide the crossfader across from the record that was playing to the new track, and you have your first mix.

Hitting that first beat

To find the first beat of the second song, listen to the track in your headphones using the Cue/PFL button.

Push and pull the record with three fingers of one hand until you have found the first beat.

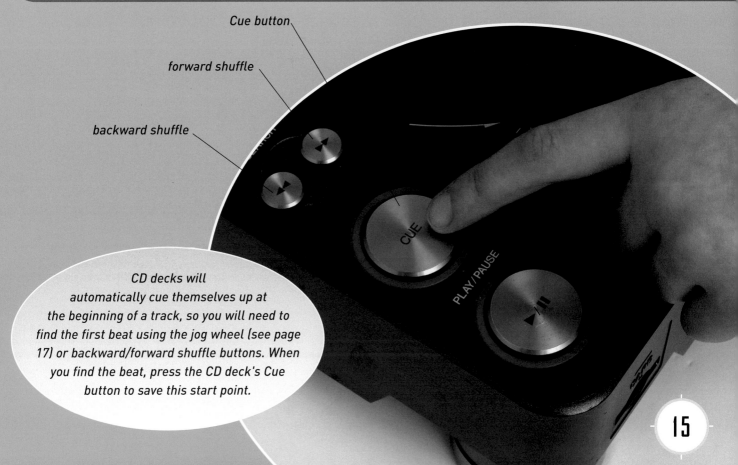

Cue button

forward shuffle

backward shuffle

CD decks will automatically cue themselves up at the beginning of a track, so you will need to find the first beat using the jog wheel (see page 17) or backward/forward shuffle buttons. When you find the beat, press the CD deck's Cue button to save this start point.

15

Beatmatching

When DJs mix together two tracks so that you cannot hear the join, they are beatmatching. It is a skill that can seem very hard at first, but can be mastered with lots of practice. There are no short cuts.

Two tracks at once

You need to get used to listening to two records at once so you can work out how to get them at the same speed. Try to listen to the headphones with one ear and the speakers with the other. Is the track in your headphones the same speed as the track coming out of the speakers?

To listen to both tracks, hold one headphone earpiece over one ear, and place the other earpiece on the side of your head or neck.

Star file

FRANKIE KNUCKLES
House music maestro

Although he first made his name as a disco DJ in 1970s New York, Frankie Knuckles shot to fame in the 1980s as one of the pioneers of house music. By then Frankie was living in Chicago, where he was a DJ at a club called The Warehouse. The electronic, disco-influenced music he played (and later made) was soon dubbed 'house' and caught the imagination of dancers around the world.

Matching the rhythms

The aim of beatmatching is to get two records in time, so that the beats sit perfectly on top of each other – in other words, they match. To do this, you will need a combination of slip-cueing (see pages 14–15) and adjusting your turntables' pitch (speed) controls.

To get the tracks in time, you can use the pitch control fader on the turntable or use your fingers to slow or speed up the spinning **platter**. When the two records are in time, you can cut and fade between the two to perform your first beatmatched mix.

*The jog wheel on a CD deck acts like the platter on a vinyl turntable. You can use it to alter the speed of the track and to carry out some **scratching** (see page 19).*

Move the pitch control fader towards you to speed up the spinning disc, and away from you to slow it down.

To manually slow down the record, hold two fingers lightly against the side of the spinning platter.

Tweaking the spindle with your thumb and fingers will speed up the record briefly.

Mixing it up

Once you can beatmatch well, you can mix records in all sorts of weird and wonderful ways. But keep things simple and remember: you are an entertainer.

Cuts and fades

Practise your cutting and fading – play around with the crossfader and upfaders and learn how small adjustments can make a big difference to the sound. Pulling the crossfader across slowly while carefully pushing up a channel fader results in a smooth, seamless mix. Doing the opposite – quick cuts and fades – can raise dancefloor energy levels, but can sometimes sound rushed.

This hip-hop DJ has turned his turntables round by 90 degrees so that the arms do not get in the way of his scratching.

EQ controls

The EQ dials are located on the mixer, above each channel fader. They will alter the **bass** and **treble**. If you turn the bass right down, you can still beatmatch by listening to the cymbals.

Counting beats

You should try to match phrases and avoid key clashes – mixing two songs that sound out of key musically. Almost all dance music follows a simple formula, with four beats to the **bar** and phrases made up of four bars. You can count beats and bars quite easily – count '1,2,3,4' then '2,2,3,4' and so on, in time with the beats. When you get to the end of the fourth bar ('4,2,3,4'), the music will change. Listen to a few records and you will hear the changes – **producers** usually leave little sound markers, such as cymbal crashes. Matching the phrases of the incoming and outgoing records will improve your mixes.

Star file

SASHA
Superstar DJ

Born Alexander Coe, Sasha was the first 'superstar DJ'. He started off in the late 1980s playing acid house records in Stoke, England. His reputation as a superb DJ soon began to spread, and by the mid-1990s, he was the world's most sought-after DJ. He was the first DJ to be treated like a rock star, with thousands flocking to see him wherever he played.

Baby scratch

The baby scratch is the easiest type of scratching. Pull the record back using three fingers of one hand.

Then push the record forwards, pull back again and repeat for as long as you want – but do not get carried away!

Your musical story

Once you have mastered the technical side of mixing, it is time to be creative. There are other important skills you will need to learn, such as choosing records and knowing when to mix. These things can turn a mediocre DJ into a great one.

Top tip

Special effects such as reverb, delay and filters can enhance your musical journey. Some mixers come with built-in effects units, or you could buy a separate unit and connect it to your normal mixer.

Try to spot the most energetic dancers on the floor. Other people will take a lead from them, so if you keep them happy and dancing, you are halfway there.

Know your stuff

First and foremost, you have to know your records. You should know how they start and end and what speed they are, as well as their structure – how they build up and what happens in them musically. If you have this information at your fingertips as you flick through your bag, you will instinctively know which records will work together. You can then use song structures to your advantage. This will help you to hit the good part of the song rather than just matching the starts and ends. As you string together records, think about the flow: how your selection builds and changes, and how dancers will react.

20

Telling a story

You can also tell stories with the records you pick. For example, you could group together songs with similar lyrics. Or you could throw in something unexpected to change direction or mood. Often 'surprise' records get the best reaction.

As you begin to play to people, you will start to understand how your choice of record can affect a dancefloor. Try to think like dancers: if you were in their shoes, what would you want to hear right now? A good way of testing out some ideas is to record a mix for your friends. This allows you to think about the pacing of a **set**, your record choice and what you are saying with the music.

When packing your bag or CD wallet, pick a variety of tracks to suit different moods. If one style of music is not going down well, you can simply pick another style from your selection.

An external effects unit can add a huge range of special effects, but it should be used sparingly – too many effects can spoil the flow of the music and put off dancers.

Playing to a crowd

Sharing great music and wowing a floor full of dancers are the attractions of DJing. The first time you play can be scary. Get it right and you will love it. More importantly, the dancers will too.

One of the crowd

The first thing to get right is your attitude. Think of yourself as one of the crowd. It is your job to make sure that everyone has fun. Try to take a mixture of tunes that are fail-safe winners, daring risks and secret weapons – those little-known records that always impress. It always pays to find out about the crowd in advance. Get to the party early to get a feel for it.

DJ equipment can vary greatly from one DJ booth to another. It is a good idea to familiarise yourself with the controls before you play your set.

Make it big, and you might find yourself playing in front of a crowd of thousands at an outdoor event, rather than in a small club. Here, the Chemical Brothers perform during a *gig* in London's Trafalgar Square in 2007.

Knowing your job

When it is your turn to play, show the previous DJ a bit of respect: do not just mix out of his last tune straight away. If you have been given an early 'warm-up' slot, try not to play too hard or fast – it is your job to ease people into the party; the energetic stuff comes later. If all goes to plan, you should soon have a dancefloor to keep an eye on. While doing this, check the sound levels – if the indicators are flashing red, turn the volume down. You may get the odd request or two from dancers, so be prepared. Be polite, however silly the request – you do not want to annoy your audience by being rude to them!

Extra items

There are a few extras you should pack in your bag. A small torch always comes in handy in dark DJ booths. If you have any **promo mix** CDs (see page 27) or business cards to give away, take those, too.

Throwing your own party

There are a lot of DJs around, so getting that first gig can sometimes be tricky. One way to ensure that you get vital experience of playing to a crowd is to arrange your own night or party.

Top tip

You should deal only with respectable venues that have a good reputation. Do not pay any money to venues in advance. Be cautious about how you promote your party on the Internet.

A properly licensed venue should provide security staff, or bouncers. They can make sure that only people with tickets can get into your party.

Party time

Throwing a party is hard work. There are lots of things to consider, including venue hire, other DJs, door security, decorations and promotion. When looking at hiring venues, it is wise to start off small. Look for somewhere with a sound system and equipment already installed, so all you have to do is get your DJs to turn up and play. You will have to cover the venue hire cost by charging admission on the door or by selling tickets in advance, so try to avoid somewhere that is expensive.

That bit extra

The best parties are usually the ones that feel 'special', so make an effort. If you get the chance to decorate the venue, do so. To make the party extra special you could even hire someone to VJ (to mix live visuals with a computer) or suggest a fancy dress theme. However great the music, it is the extra touches that people remember.

Finally, make sure that people know about your party by promoting it. But be careful – invites to parties and events can get out of hand and you should make sure that you know everyone who is going to turn up.

Try to decorate your venue using lighting and effects, such as glitterballs. Even a few balloons can make a difference.

Promoting your party

1

You need to make sure people know about the party. Posters and fliers are traditional methods used.

2

You can also promote on the Internet, using messageboards and social networking sites – but ask an adult first.

Self-promotion

Most people who take up DJing dream of making it big, but the truth is that very few become superstars. However, if you are DJing because you love music, then this should not put you off.

Getting out there

There are plenty of things you can do to help get yourself gigs. You should go and find other people who like similar records to you. Meet other DJs and introduce yourself – being part of the 'scene' helps you pick up bookings and make contacts.

Your local music shop is a great location to meet and talk to DJs. It is also the place to find the latest releases and that occasional classic tune.

Star file

FATBOY SLIM
Brighton beatmaster

Norman Cook, best known as Fatboy Slim, is arguably the most successful dance music DJ and producer of all time. He has had huge success in the UK singles charts, first as a member of The Housemartins, and then with Freak Power, Beats International and as Fatboy Slim. He remains one of the most sought-after DJs in the world, and once played to a crowd of over 200,000 in his home town of Brighton, England.

Getting noticed

To get noticed, you will need to promote yourself. Building up your profile by starting your own Internet radio station (see below) and by posting regular DJ charts of your favourite records will help get you onto promo lists. You will then receive free copies of tracks before they are released commercially. In truth, very few DJs get free records, but if you are a working DJ with regular gigs, you stand a very good chance. If you are lucky enough to get on a list, you will need to fill out regular reaction sheets to stay on it.

Promo CDs and records

Promo CDs are an easy way for potential clients to hear your music and to get your name known.

Promo records come with a reaction sheet – sending these back will ensure you keep getting free discs.

Using the Internet

Launching your own Internet radio station is a great way of building up a fan base. All you need is some webcast software, a microphone and a broadband Internet connection.

Top tip

If you decide to make your own promotional mix CDs, make them look as professional as possible. Including artwork, a track list and contact details will help get bookings.

Taking it further

The best method of getting yourself noticed is to start making your own edits, remixes and tracks. This is a great way of developing your skills and, more importantly, making your DJ sets unique.

Re-edits

You should consider getting into music production only when you have a reasonable amount of experience of playing in front of audiences. The first step into music production for most DJs is making their own **re-edits**. These are customised versions of existing records, where you use music-editing software to rearrange the song. DJs have been doing this since the 1970s, and most of the top DJs still make their own versions of tracks.

Top tip

If you decide to make your own music, you might be able to get it released. There are many 'digital only' MP3 music labels that specialise in releasing new dance music from up-and-coming young producers.

Music-editing software will display music tracks as sound waves. You can then cut up these tracks and paste together the bits you want to create your own music.

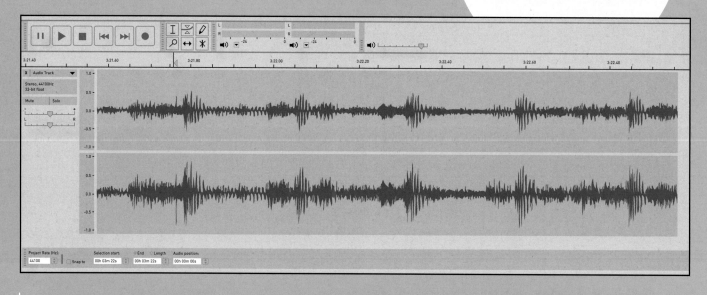

Mixing things up

The basic idea of a re-edit is to take a song you like and make it more 'dancefloor-friendly'. This may mean extending certain drum passages, taking out vocal sections or looping up (repeating) parts of the song that people like to dance to. To do your own edits, you will need to use some music-editing software. There are a number of very good software packages available for free. Learning to make edits takes time, but it is time well spent – not only will you have a load of personalised versions of your favourite music tracks, but you will also have picked up the basics of music production.

Over time, you can build up collections of different re-edits to suit different occasions and venues.

 Glossary

acid house a genre of house music with a repetitive, hypnotic style.

amplifier a device that changes the amplitude, or volume, of a sound.

bar a segment of music made up of a set number of beats. Usually the first beat in each bar is slightly accented.

bass the low tones in a piece of music, usually including a drum beat.

booth the desk where a DJ can set up equipment and store CDs and records.

CD decks a device, usually with features such as a jog wheel, used by DJs to play CDs.

channel music from a single source, such as a turntable or a CD deck.

crossfader the control on a mixer that moves the speaker output from one source, or channel, to another.

genre the musical type. Dance music is made up of lots of genres, such as hip-hop and funk.

gig a job or event where a DJ is hired to play.

ground wire a thin wire that connects a turntable to the mixer and prevents the build-up of static electricity that would spoil the sound quality.

jog wheel the control on a CD deck used to find the first beat and to perform scratching.

looped-up when part of a song is repeated over and over again to form a loop.

mix blending different tracks together so that they make a seamless passage of music.

mixer the device used by DJs to blend together music from more than one source.

MP3s a computer file used for music.

platter the spinning mat that holds the vinyl record on a turntable.

producers the person who oversees the recording and mixing of records.

promo mix a recorded sample of a DJ's work that is used to advertise their skills.

re-edits individual versions of existing tunes that are put together using computer software.

scratching when a DJ moves a turntable platter or CD deck jog wheel back and forth to create a scratching sound effect.

set the period of time when a DJ plays his or her music mixes.

socket an attachment point for the wires of electrical devices.

stylus the needle on the end of the turntable arm. The needle reads the grooves on a vinyl record and translates them into sounds.

track an individual tune.

treble the higher tones in a piece of music.

turntable a device used to play vinyl records.

upfaders the controls on the mixer that change the volume from individual sources, or channels.

USB (Universal Serial Bus) a connection used to link computers to pieces of equipment.

vinyl records flat discs made from a type of plastic. They have tiny grooves on their surface that are read by a stylus.

DJing organisations

There are several organisations and associations that offer advice and support to professional DJs.

The National Association of Disc Jockeys offers advice, training and contacts, as well as putting on regular sales of secondhand equipment and circulating a monthly magazine.

The British DJ Organisation offers technical and legal advice to DJs in Great Britain.

The Players Association is an online radio station that allows DJs to upload mixes so that they can be listened to by music-lovers around the world.

Further reading

There are plenty of books available for the newcomer as well as the more experienced DJ.

How to DJ (Properly): The Art and Science of Playing Records Brewster, Bill and Broughton, Frank (Bantam Press, 2006)

DJing for Dummies Steventon, John (John Wiley & Sons, 2006)

DJ Skills: The Essential Guide to Mixing and Scratching Webber, Stephen (Focal Press, 2007)

How to DJ Wood, Rob (Teach Yourself, 2005)

Websites

The Internet is a great place for information on techniques and advice, as well as forums where DJs share their mixing wisdom.

www.i-dj.co.uk

The website of I-DJ magazine comes with reviews of the latest equipment, interviews with some of the biggest DJ names and tutorials for essential skills.

www.nadj.org.uk

Home of the National Association of Disc Jockeys, it offers advice to professional DJs.

www.residentadvisor.net

DJing news, views and forums from around the world.

Index